In days of old

A round 700 years ago, Europe was dotted with high-walled stone forts and castles.

At this time the people of Europe were ruled by a number of different kings and powerful nobles who were always fighting each other. Castles provided them with a safe place from which to rule their lands.

Why build castles?

C astles were built to defend towns or river crossings. They had to be difficult to attack and big enough to shelter a small army. Then if a nobleman's lands were invaded he and his men could retreat there.

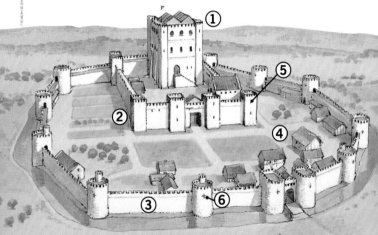

KEY TO THE CASTLE

① The keep was the strongest part of all.

② Towers strengthened the inner walls.

③ The outer wall guarded people and animals.

④ The bailey could shelter many people.

⑤ Slits in the wall let archers shoot out.

⑥ Crossbowmen fired from cross-shaped slits in the walls.

LITTLE LIBRARY

Castles

Christopher Maynard

Kingfisher Books

Contents

Castles were more than just a strong-hold for soldiers, however. They were also a home for the lord's family and all their servants. More than 50 people might live in a castle.

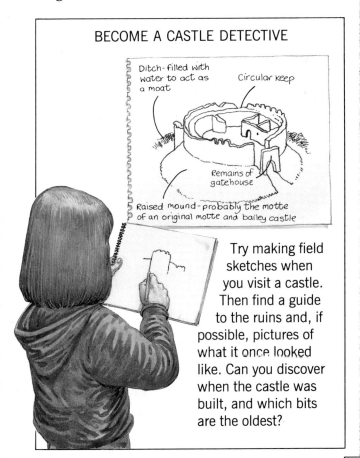

BECOME A CASTLE DETECTIVE

Ditch-filled with water to act as a moat

Circular keep

Remains of gatehouse

Raised mound-probably the motte of an original motte and bailey castle

Try making field sketches when you visit a castle. Then find a guide to the ruins and, if possible, pictures of what it once looked like. Can you discover when the castle was built, and which bits are the oldest?

Castles of wood

The first castles were built about 900 years ago. They were called motte and bailey castles.

The motte was a high earth mound. On top stood a wooden tower which was the strongest part of the castle. The bailey was an open area which was ringed by a high fence, or palisade.

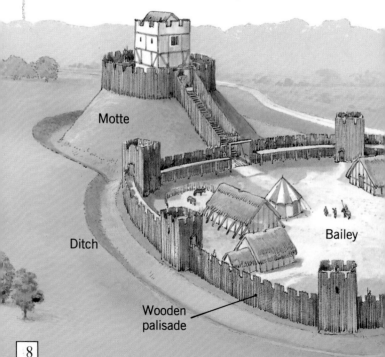

Motte

Ditch

Bailey

Wooden palisade

MAKE A MOTTE AND BAILEY CASTLE

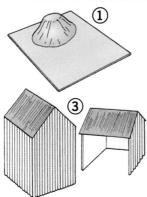

①

② Sticky tape

③

④ Attach with cotton

1 Make a motte out of plasticene or papier mâché and put it on a board.
2 Use straws held together by sticky tape to make walls.

3 Make buildings out of some empty milk cartons. Glue straws to the sides of them.
4 Cover a cardboard square with straws for a drawbridge.

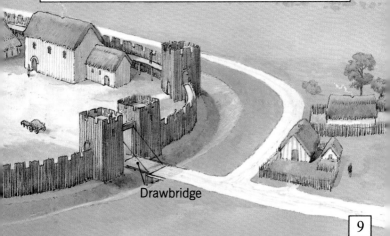

Drawbridge

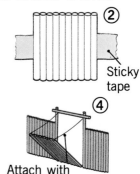

Castles of stone

The problem with wooden castles was that they could easily be set on fire. Stone gave more protection, but it was also a lot more expensive.

If a nobleman or knight was rich enough, he could build a stone castle that was almost impossible to capture. He could make the walls as thick or as high as he wanted. If a knight was poor and could not afford a castle, he might build a fortified manor house. With stone walls around it, the house could be defended by just a few men.

Some castles were no more than a single stone tower called a keep. They had very thick walls, and were as high as 35 metres. Sometimes the main door was well above the ground to make it harder to break in.

The land around the castle was owned by the lord. It was farmed by workers known as peasants, but they were not paid for their work. Instead, they were given small plots of land on which they could grow their own food. The lord also protected them in times of trouble.

Curtain walls

Over the years the design of castles changed, and people started to build castles with a set of double walls. These were known as curtain walls.

If attackers smashed through the outer curtain wall, the defenders could move back behind the inner one. Often the inner wall was higher than the outer, so two lines of soldiers could fire arrows at the enemy.

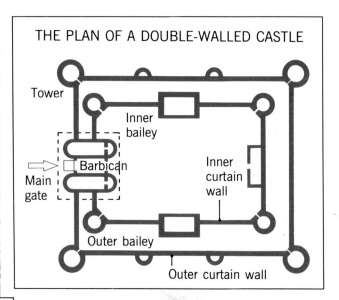

THE PLAN OF A DOUBLE-WALLED CASTLE

Tower

Inner bailey

Barbican

Main gate

Inner curtain wall

Outer bailey

Outer curtain wall

KEY TO THE BARBICAN

① Archers fired arrows down on their attackers.

② A drawbridge was raised to block the main gate.

③ A portcullis barred the entrance.

④ Murder holes were used to drop hot sand and rocks on to attackers.

⑤ Archers fired down through wall slits.

⑥ Archers on the inner wall fired over the lower one.

Building a castle

A really big castle could take ten years to complete, and needed an army of builders. A master mason was in charge. He planned everything – just like an architect does today. Masons shaped and fitted the huge stones, and carpenters cut the wood. The peasants did the digging and carrying.

Logs were cut into even planks over a deep sawpit.

Masons used mallets and chisels to cut blocks of stone that fitted well.

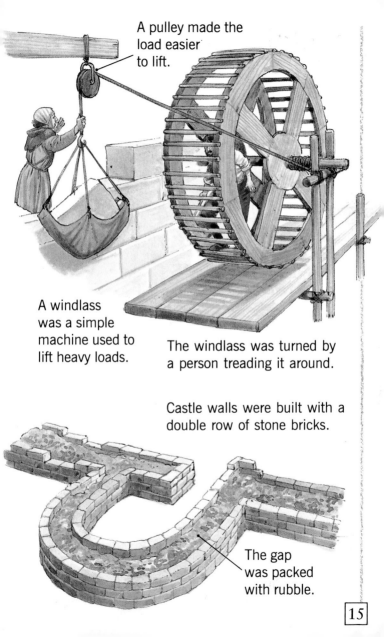

A pulley made the load easier to lift.

A windlass was a simple machine used to lift heavy loads.

The windlass was turned by a person treading it around.

Castle walls were built with a double row of stone bricks.

The gap was packed with rubble.

15

Living in a castle

A castle was just like a small town, with its own carpenters, priests, blacksmiths and stablemen. There were servants to care for the lord and his family, also soldiers, grooms and huntsmen. A wealthy lord might own several castles. He and his family would spend a few months at each one in turn.

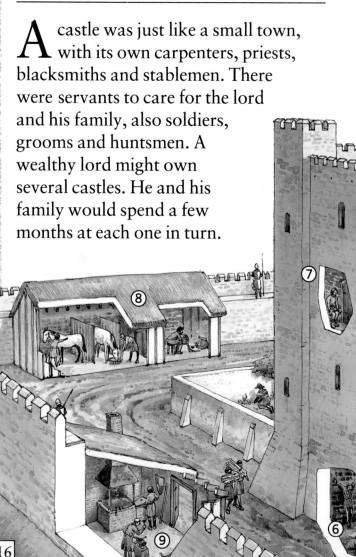

KEY TO THE CASTLE

1. Spiral staircase
2. Lord's bedroom
3. Chapel
4. Great Hall
5. Kitchen
6. Storeroom (also used as dungeon)
7. Toilet
8. Stables
9. Blacksmith

Food and feasts

A ll the meals were prepared in a huge kitchen in the cellars. There the cooks produced enormous feasts for the lord and his guests. In the kitchen was a roaring fire over which pots of water were boiled and meat was grilled. The fireplace was big enough to roast a whole pig.

CASTLE CAKES

Here is a dish you might have eaten at a castle. You need: 175 grams dried figs, $\frac{1}{2}$ tsp powdered cloves, $\frac{1}{2}$ tsp ground black pepper, 1 dsp honey, a pinch of saffron, 225 grams of shortcrust pastry, a greased baking tray.

1 Cut up the figs and mix with the cloves, pepper, honey and saffron in a bowl.

2 Roll out the pastry and cut out rounds. Put some fig mixture on to each round.

3 Dampen the edges of the rounds with water. Fold and press the edges together.

4 Bake cakes for 20 minutes in preheated oven at 200°C or Gas Mark 6 until they are golden brown.

5 Heat 4 tablespoons of honey with 4 of water. Pour the syrup over the cakes and serve.

A tournament

K nights spent a long time training to fight. Apart from fighting in battles, the best place to test their skills was at a tournament. At these mock fights the knights always used blunt weapons. Tournaments were held on holidays, or when the lord had visitors to entertain.

MAKE A KNIGHT'S HELMET

①   ②   ③

A ✛   ✛ B

1 Cut out a sheet of card so it is big enough to fit comfortably around your head.
2 Cut short tabs on one long side and fold them down. Cut a card circle to fit on top.
3 Glue the top of the helmet on to the tabs. Then mark points A and B on each side.

④  ⑤  ⑥

4 Cut out a vizor deep enough to cover your face and wide enough to reach from A to B.
5 Fasten the vizor to the helmet at A and B with brass paper fasteners. Cover the inside ends of the fasteners with tape.
6 Cut paper sheets into strips. Roll them into a plume and fasten with tape. Make a hole in the helmet top. Push the base of your plume through and tape into place.

Attacking a castle

Capturing a castle was hard work. If there was no way to get in by trickery, the only choice left was to attack the castle. Soldiers would try to break through the main gate with a battering ram, while others fought to climb the walls with scaling ladders. The rest of the army fired arrows and crossbow bolts.

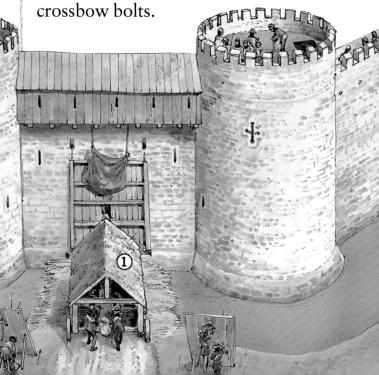

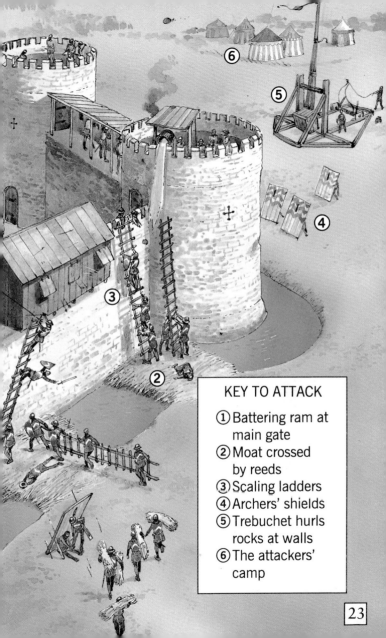

KEY TO ATTACK

① Battering ram at main gate
② Moat crossed by reeds
③ Scaling ladders
④ Archers' shields
⑤ Trebuchet hurls rocks at walls
⑥ The attackers' camp

23

Laying siege

If a castle was too strong to storm, the attackers could lay siege to it and weaken the defenders. They used siege engines to batter down the walls. They also tried to starve the people inside by stopping any food getting in.

▷ A ballista was a giant crossbow that was used to hurl rocks at castle walls.

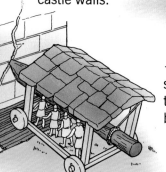

◁ A roof covered with animal skins protected soldiers as they swung an iron-tipped battering ram at the castle.

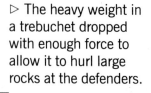

▷ The heavy weight in a trebuchet dropped with enough force to allow it to hurl large rocks at the defenders.

MAKE YOUR OWN SIEGE CATAPULT

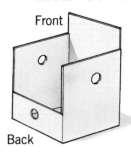

Front

Back

1 Cut the top off a milk carton to make this shape. Cut out holes in both sides and at the back as shown.

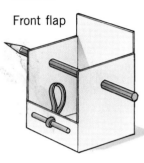

Front flap

2 Thread a small elastic band through the back hole and fix it in place with a used matchstick. Push a long pencil through both holes in the sides.

3 Cut a matchbox tray in half and tape it to another pencil. Loop the elastic band over the end of this pencil. Fold and tape the front flap down.

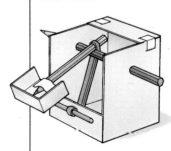

4 Put a pellet of paper inside the matchbox, pull back and fire!

25

The fall of castles

About 500 years ago castles began to be less useful. This was because armies started to use gunpowder and cannons. With these, they could batter down any castle walls, no matter how thick or high they were.

Also as kings became more powerful, the nobles no longer needed the safety of their cold castles. They began to live in large houses instead.

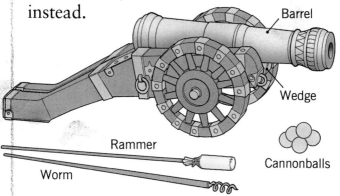

Barrel

Wedge

Rammer

Worm

Cannonballs

The first cannons used a rammer to pack gunpowder and cannonballs into the barrel. A worm was used to clear out the barrel after it was fired. The barrel was raised and lowered with a wedge that was pushed underneath it.

During the English Civil War of 1642–1648, castles were again used as strongholds. The defenders fired their guns from positions outside the castle walls.

When Oliver Cromwell, leader of Parliament's forces, captured a castle held by Royalists he blew up the walls with gunpowder so it could never be used again.

Castles today

Most of the castles still standing today are in ruins. If you visit them, you have to look hard for clues that show what they were once like.

One way is to make a plan of the castle as you walk around it. First draw in the walls and towers and main gate. Then try to work out where the main rooms would have been.

The ruins below, and the complete castle on the opposite page, show some of the main features to look out for.

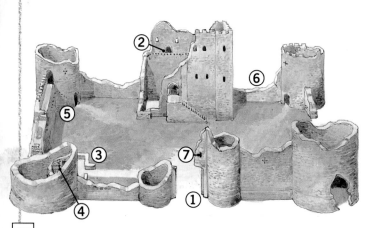

DISCOVERING RUINED CASTLES

The ruin opposite was once a splendid castle. Here are seven clues to help you understand castle ruins better.

1 Grooves in the gatehouse wall show where the portcullis once fitted.

2 Fireplaces and holes for beams show each floor level.

3 The shape of some rooms can be seen from the remains of their foundations.

4 The remains of spiral staircases may be seen inside many towers.

5 Lines of stones, or stains, will show where other buildings used to lean against the castle walls.

6 The remains of walls will show how high and thick they once were.

7 Holes in the wall near the main gate show where the chains of a draw-bridge once ran.

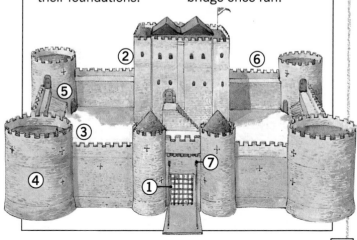

Index

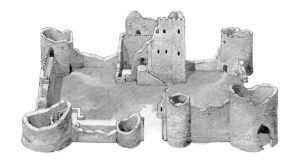